HANDWRITING PRACTICE FOR KIDS
Children's Reading & Writing Education Books

All Rights reserved. No part of this book may be reproduced or used in any way or form or by any means whether electronic or mechanical, this means that you cannot record or photocopy any material ideas or tips that are provided in this book

Copyright 2016

Trace and rewrite the words.

above

Trace the word and read the word out loud.

above   above   above

Write the word and read the word out loud.

Trace the word and read the word out loud.

above   above   above

Write the word and read the word out loud.

FORM A SENTENCE USING THE WORD ABOVE.

absent

Trace the word and read the word out loud.

absent absent absent

Write the word and read the word out loud.

Trace the word and read the word out loud.

absent absent absent

Write the word and read the word out loud.

FORM A SENTENCE USING THE WORD ABOVE.

beat

Trace the word and read the word out loud.

beat   beat   beat

Write the word and read the word out loud.

Trace the word and read the word out loud.

beat   *beat*   *beat*

Write the word and read the word out loud.

FORM A SENTENCE USING THE WORD ABOVE.

before

Trace the word and read the word out loud.

before before before

Write the word and read the word out loud.

Trace the word and read the word out loud.

before before before

Write the word and read the word out loud.

FORM A SENTENCE USING THE WORD ABOVE.

call

Trace the word and read the word out loud.

call   call   call

Write the word and read the word out loud.

Trace the word and read the word out loud.

call   *call*   *call*

Write the word and read the word out loud.

FORM A SENTENCE USING THE WORD ABOVE.

carry

Trace the word and read the word out loud.

carry   carry   carry

Write the word and read the word out loud.

Trace the word and read the word out loud.

carry   carry   carry

Write the word and read the word out loud.

FORM A SENTENCE USING THE WORD ABOVE.

dirty

Trace the word and read the word out loud.

dirty   dirty   dirty

Write the word and read the word out loud.

Trace the word and read the word out loud.

dirty   *dirty*   *dirty*

Write the word and read the word out loud.

FORM A SENTENCE USING THE WORD ABOVE.

dozen

Trace the word and read the word out loud.

dozen   dozen   dozen

Write the word and read the word out loud.

Trace the word and read the word out loud.

dozen   *dozen*   *dozen*

Write the word and read the word out loud.

FORM A SENTENCE USING THE WORD ABOVE.

early

Trace the word and read the word out loud.

early   early   early

Write the word and read the word out loud.

Trace the word and read the word out loud.

early   *early*   *early*

Write the word and read the word out loud.

FORM A SENTENCE USING THE WORD ABOVE.

effect

Trace the word and read the word out loud.

effect effect effect

Write the word and read the word out loud.

Trace the word and read the word out loud.

effect effect effect

Write the word and read the word out loud.

FORM A SENTENCE USING THE WORD ABOVE.

frozen

Trace the word and read the word out loud.

frozen   frozen   frozen

Write the word and read the word out loud.

Trace the word and read the word out loud.

frozen   frozen   frozen

Write the word and read the word out loud.

FORM A SENTENCE USING THE WORD ABOVE.

feel

Trace the word and read the word out loud.

feel   feel   feel

Write the word and read the word out loud.

Trace the word and read the word out loud.

feel   *feel*   *feel*

Write the word and read the word out loud.

FORM A SENTENCE USING THE WORD ABOVE.

goal

Trace the word and read the word out loud.

goal   goal   goal

Write the word and read the word out loud.

Trace the word and read the word out loud.

goal   *goal*   *goal*

Write the word and read the word out loud.

FORM A SENTENCE USING THE WORD ABOVE.

guest

Trace the word and read the word out loud.

guest   guest   guest

Write the word and read the word out loud.

Trace the word and read the word out loud.

guest   *guest*   *guest*

Write the word and read the word out loud.

FORM A SENTENCE USING THE WORD ABOVE.

half

Trace the word and read the word out loud.

half   half   half

Write the word and read the word out loud.

Trace the word and read the word out loud.

half   *half*   *half*

Write the word and read the word out loud.

FORM A SENTENCE USING THE WORD ABOVE.

heal

Trace the word and read the word out loud.

heal   heal   heal

Write the word and read the word out loud.

Trace the word and read the word out loud.

heal   *heal*   *heal*

Write the word and read the word out loud.

FORM A SENTENCE USING THE WORD ABOVE.

item

Trace the word and read the word out loud.

item   item   item

Write the word and read the word out loud.

Trace the word and read the word out loud.

item   *item*   *item*

Write the word and read the word out loud.

FORM A SENTENCE USING THE WORD ABOVE.

join

Trace the word and read the word out loud.

join join join

Write the word and read the word out loud.

Trace the word and read the word out loud.

join *join* *join*

Write the word and read the word out loud.

FORM A SENTENCE USING THE WORD ABOVE.

keep

Trace the word and read the word out loud.

keep   keep   keep

Write the word and read the word out loud.

Trace the word and read the word out loud.

keep   *keep*   *keep*

Write the word and read the word out loud.

FORM A SENTENCE USING THE WORD ABOVE.

kind

Trace the word and read the word out loud.

kind kind kind

Write the word and read the word out loud.

Trace the word and read the word out loud.

kind *kind* *kind*

Write the word and read the word out loud.

FORM A SENTENCE USING THE WORD ABOVE.

lack

Trace the word and read the word out loud.

lack　　　lack　　　lack

Write the word and read the word out loud.

Trace the word and read the word out loud.

lack　　　*lack*　　　*lack*

Write the word and read the word out loud.

FORM A SENTENCE USING THE WORD ABOVE.

main

Trace the word and read the word out loud.

main   main   main

Write the word and read the word out loud.

Trace the word and read the word out loud.

main   main   main

Write the word and read the word out loud.

FORM A SENTENCE USING THE WORD ABOVE.

near

Trace the word and read the word out loud.

near near near

Write the word and read the word out loud.

Trace the word and read the word out loud.

near *near* *near*

Write the word and read the word out loud.

FORM A SENTENCE USING THE WORD ABOVE.

once

Trace the word and read the word out loud.

once   once   once

Write the word and read the word out loud.

Trace the word and read the word out loud.

once   *once*   *once*

Write the word and read the word out loud.

FORM A SENTENCE USING THE WORD ABOVE.

plan

Trace the word and read the word out loud.

plan   plan   plan

Write the word and read the word out loud.

Trace the word and read the word out loud.

plan   *plan*   *plan*

Write the word and read the word out loud.

FORM A SENTENCE USING THE WORD ABOVE.

quit

Trace the word and read the word out loud.

quit   quit   quit

Write the word and read the word out loud.

Trace the word and read the word out loud.

quit   *quit*   *quit*

Write the word and read the word out loud.

FORM A SENTENCE USING THE WORD ABOVE.

read

Trace the word and read the word out loud.

read read read

Write the word and read the word out loud.

Trace the word and read the word out loud.

read *read* *read*

Write the word and read the word out loud.

FORM A SENTENCE USING THE WORD ABOVE.

secret

Trace the word and read the word out loud.

secret   secret   secret

Write the word and read the word out loud.

Trace the word and read the word out loud.

secret   secret   secret

Write the word and read the word out loud.

FORM A SENTENCE USING THE WORD ABOVE.

taste

Trace the word and read the word out loud.

taste   taste   taste

Write the word and read the word out loud.

Trace the word and read the word out loud.

taste   *taste*   *taste*

Write the word and read the word out loud.

FORM A SENTENCE USING THE WORD ABOVE.

type

Trace the word and read the word out loud.

type   type   type

Write the word and read the word out loud.

Trace the word and read the word out loud.

type   *type*   *type*

Write the word and read the word out loud.

FORM A SENTENCE USING THE WORD ABOVE.

unable

Trace the word and read the word out loud.

unable unable unable

Write the word and read the word out loud.

Trace the word and read the word out loud.

unable unable unable

Write the word and read the word out loud.

FORM A SENTENCE USING THE WORD ABOVE.

version

Trace the word and read the word out loud.

version version version

Write the word and read the word out loud.

Trace the word and read the word out loud.

version version version

Write the word and read the word out loud.

FORM A SENTENCE USING THE WORD ABOVE.

want

Trace the word and read the word out loud.

want   want   want

Write the word and read the word out loud.

Trace the word and read the word out loud.

want   want   want

Write the word and read the word out loud.

FORM A SENTENCE USING THE WORD ABOVE.

x-ray

Trace the word and read the word out loud.

x-ray x-ray x-ray

Write the word and read the word out loud.

Trace the word and read the word out loud.

x-ray x-ray x-ray

Write the word and read the word out loud.

FORM A SENTENCE USING THE WORD ABOVE.

yellow

Trace the word and read the word out loud.

yellow yellow yellow

Write the word and read the word out loud.

Trace the word and read the word out loud.

yellow yellow yellow

Write the word and read the word out loud.

FORM A SENTENCE USING THE WORD ABOVE.

zero

Trace the word and read the word out loud.

zero   zero   zero

Write the word and read the word out loud.

Trace the word and read the word out loud.

zero   *zero*   *zero*

Write the word and read the word out loud.

FORM A SENTENCE USING THE WORD ABOVE.

www.ingramcontent.com/pod-product-compliance
Lightning Source LLC
LaVergne TN
LVHW082253070426
835507LV00034B/2277